We're from China

Emma Lynch

Heinemann Library
Chicago, Illinois

Customer Service 888-454-2279
Visit our website at www.heinemannlibrary.com

Editorial: Jilly Attwood, Kate Bellamy, Adam Miller
Design: Ron Kamen, Celia Jones
Picture research: Maria Joannou, Erica Newbery
Photographer: Debbie Rowe
Production: Severine Ribierre

Originated by Ambassador Litho Ltd
Printed and bound in China by South China Printing Company Ltd

09 08 07 06 05
10 9 8 7 6 5 4 3 2 1

Library of Congress Cataloging-in-Publication Data
Lynch, Emma.
  We're from China / Emma Lynch.
     p. cm. -- (We're from ...)
  Includes bibliographical references and index.
  ISBN 1-4034-5803-0 (lib. Binding-hardcover)
  ISBN 1-4034-5812-X (pbk.)
  1. China--Social life and customs--2002---Juvenile literature. 2. Children--China--Juvenile literature. 3. Family--China--Juvenile literature. I. Title. II. Series: We're from.
  DS779.43.L96 2005
  951.06--dc22

                          2005002676

Acknowledgements
The publishers would like to thank the following for permission to reproduce photographs:
Corbis p. **30c** (royalty free); Harcourt Education pp. **1, 5a, 5b, 6a, 6b, 7, 8a, 8b, 9a, 9b, 10a, 10b, 11, 12a, 12b, 13, 14a, 14b, 15a, 15b, 16a, 16b, 17a, 17b, 18, 19a, 19b, 20, 21a, 21b, 22a, 22b, 23a, 23b, 24, 25, 26a, 26b, 27, 28a, 28b, 29, 30a, 30b** (Debbie Rowe).

Cover photograph of Liu Jiasi and classmates, reproduced with permission of Harcourt Education Ltd/Debbie Rowe.

Many thanks to Liu Jiasi, Tao Kui, Thomas, and their families.

Every effort has been made to contact copyright holders of any material reproduced in this book. Any omissions will be rectified in subsequent printings if notice is given to the publishers. The paper used to print this book comes from sustainable sources.

Contents

Some words are shown in bold, **like this**. You can find out what they mean by looking in the glossary.

Where Is China?

To learn more about China we meet three children who live there. China is in Asia. China is the fourth largest country in the world.

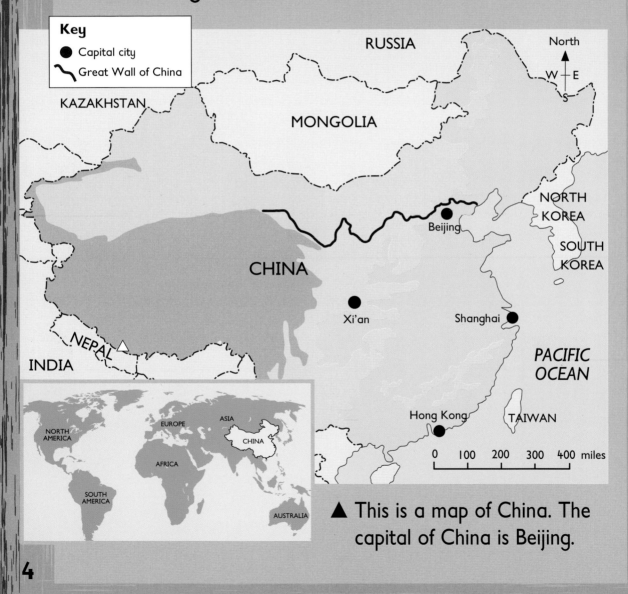

Key
- ● Capital city
- ⌇ Great Wall of China

RUSSIA

North
W—E
S

KAZAKHSTAN

MONGOLIA

CHINA

NORTH KOREA

Beijing

SOUTH KOREA

Xi'an

Shanghai

NEPAL

INDIA

PACIFIC OCEAN

Hong Kong

TAIWAN

0   100   200   300   400 miles

NORTH AMERICA

EUROPE

ASIA

CHINA

AFRICA

SOUTH AMERICA

AUSTRALIA

▲ This is a map of China. The capital of China is Beijing.

Northern China is very cold. Southern China is very warm. China has many mountains. Most people live in eastern China, where the land is lower.

More people live in ▶ China than any other country of the world.

▲ China has mountains and hills, grasslands, and **deserts**.

Meet Liu Jiasi

Liu Jiasi is six years old. She lives in an apartment in Beijing with her mother and father. Liu Jiasi's parents work at the university in Beijing.

Liu Jiasi's father

Liu Jiasi's mother

Liu Jiasi

▲ Liu Jiasi's favorite food is tomato and egg soup.

In the evenings the family eats together. Liu Jiasi's mother cooks. Sometimes they go out to eat.

At School

Liu Jiasi goes to school five days a week. She lives near her school, so she walks there. She studies Chinese, physical education, science, math, and painting.

▼ There are 40 children in Liu Jiasi's class. Her best friend is Liu Jing.

Liu Jiasi likes painting, science, and math. She wants to be a scientist when she grows up. Liu Jiasi does not like physical education.

▼ Students at Liu Jiasi's school do exercises outside.

Having Fun

At home, Liu Jiasi likes to play with her toys and draw. She also enjoys riding her bike. Sometimes she and her parents visit the park.

▼ Liu Jiasi enjoys trips out in Beijing.

Liu Jiasi looks forward to the New Year celebrations. At New Year, families give their children presents of money in red envelopes. These envelopes are called **hong bao**.

City and Country

Cities such as Beijing are big and full of people. There are lots of taxis, buses, and trucks. People go to work in offices and visit shops.

Life in town is ▶ noisy and busy.

The countryside is much quieter. There are not many cars or trucks. Families live together or very near each other in villages.

In the country, people ▶ work on the land and grow their own food.

Meet Tao Kui

Tao Kui is seven years old. He lives in a house in a farming village. His parents are farmers. They grow rice, **water chestnuts**, and squash.

Tao Kui's mother

Tao Kui's grandfather

Tao Kui's grandmother

Tao Kui's father

Tao Kui

▲ Tao Kui lives with his mother, father, and grandparents.

Tao Kui would ▶
like to be a
farmer, like
his father.

Tao Kui's aunts and uncles also live in
the village. He visits them often. He
likes to play outside because there is
so much space.

Daily Life

Tao Kui goes to school. He also helps the family with their work. He walks the water buffaloes to the water, so they do not get too hot.

◀ Sometimes Tao Kui goes swimming.

chopsticks

▲ Tao Kui's family uses **chopsticks** to eat their food.

The family grows a lot of the food they eat. They buy the rest of their food from the market. Tao Kui likes eating fish, but he does not like spicy food.

Playtime

Tao Kui has a new puppy to play with. He also has lots of friends who live nearby. They play outside all the time because it is very hot.

▲ Tao Kui has a new friend!

Tao Kui and his friends like to climb
trees, go swimming, and ride their
bikes. They have to be careful because
there are lots of snakes in the area.

Art, Music and Theater

China is famous for making pictures of plants and animals on pottery, paper, and silk. People also paint Chinese signs on special paper or silk. This art is called **calligraphy**.

▲ This boy is learning calligraphy.

▼ Chinese opera is a mixture of singing, acting, acrobatics, and music.

Lots of Chinese people enjoy theater, music, and dance. There are lots of art **festivals**. Many Chinese people like Chinese opera, too.

Meet Thomas

Thomas is eight years old. He lives in a tall apartment building in Hong Kong. Thomas' parents are out at work all day. When Thomas finishes school, a maid takes care of him.

Thomas's mother

Thomas's grandmothers

Thomas's father

Thomas

▲ Thomas lives with his mother, father, and their maid.

▲ Some people do **tai chi** in the garden by the flats.

Lots of people live in the same block of flats as Thomas' family. His family shares a garden with the other people who live in their apartment building.

Having Fun

Thomas has lots of fun after school. He likes reading, playing with building bricks, and doing **tae kwon do**.

▲ Thomas is dressed for tae kwon do.

▼ Sometimes Thomas and his parents go on boat trips to the islands near Hong Kong.

Thomas also enjoys days out with his parents. They visit the park or the beach. They have barbecues and visit museums. They have even been on a helicopter tour!

School and Play

Thomas goes to school every day on the bus. He has lots of friends at school. His best friend is Tommy Lam. Tommy is very smart.

▼ Thomas wears a school uniform.

After school, Thomas and his friends
play at the playground. They wear
play shorts and T-shirts. Thomas
wears new clothes for the Chinese
New Year celebrations.

China's History

China has a very long and important history. This army of clay soldiers and horses is in a museum at Xi'an. The clay army is over 2,000 years old.

◀ Every soldier looks slightly different.

▼ Many tourists visit the Great
Wall of China every year.

The Great Wall of China was built
more than 2,000 years ago. It was built
to keep China's enemies out. It is so
long it can be seen from space!

Chinese Fact File

Flag **Capital city** **Money**

Beijing Yuan

Religion
• Most people in China do not follow a religion, but a small number of people are Taoist, Buddhist, Muslim, or Christian.

Language
• There are many languages and dialects in China, including Mandarin, Cantonese or Putonghua.

Try speaking Mandarin!
ni hao .... Hello.
wo jiao... My name is…
xie xie... Thank you.

Glossary

calligraphy beautiful handwriting done with a special pen or brush

chopsticks two special sticks used to eat food with instead of knives and forks. They are held in one hand.

desert very hot, dry area of land that has almost no rain and very few plants

festival big celebration for a town or country

hong bao means "red package" in Chinese

tai chi gentle movements and breathing exercises to help people feel calm

tae kwon do sport that uses balancing and kicking skills

university where people go to continue learning when they finish school

water chestnut plant that grows in water. Peaple eat the underground stem, It tastes a bit like a nut.

More Books to Read

Harvey, Miles. *Look What Came From China!* Danbury, Conn,: Franklin Watts, 1999.

Krach, Maywen Shen. *D is for Doufu: An Alphabet Book of Chinese Culture.* Fremont, Calif.: Shen's Books, 2000.

Simonds, Nina, Leslie Swartz, and the Children's Museum Boston. *A Treasury of Chinese Holiday Tales, Activities, and Recipes.* Orlando, Fla.: Gulliver Books, 2002.

Index